THE ETHICS OF WAR

Patience Coster

W
FRANKLIN WATTS
LONDON·SYDNEY

Paperback edition first published in 2014 by Franklin Watts

Franklin Watts
338 Euston Road
London
NW1 3BH

Franklin Watts Australia
Level 17/207 Kent Street, Sydney, NSW 2000

Produced by Arcturus Publishing Limited,
26/27 Bickels Yard, 151–153 Bermondsey Street, London SE1 3HA

Editors: Nicola Barber and Joe Harris
Picture researcher: Nicola Barber
Designer: Ian Winton

Picture credits:
Corbis: 13 (Bettmann), 14 (Rick Maiman/Sygma), 22 (David J. & Janice L. Frent Collection), 29 (Bettmann), 33 (Roger Hutchings/In Pictures), 34 (Bettmann). Shutterstock: cover left (LSqrd42), cover right (Przemek Tokar), title page and 25 (Pedro Jorge Henriques Monteiro), 7 (Ken Tannenbaum), 8 (kenny1), 10 left (danileon), 10 right (Goran Bogicevic), 17 (Patrick Poendl), 18 and 21 (Northfoto), 27 (L. Kragt Bakker), 31 (Oleg Yarko), 37 (Rena Schild), 38 (brandonht), 41 (Northfoto), 43 (jan kranendonk).

British Library Cataloguing in Publication Data

Coster, Patience.
   The ethics of war. -- (Both sides of the story)
   1. War--Moral and ethical aspects--Juvenile literature.
   I. Title II. Series III. Barber, Nicola.
   172.4'2-dc23

ISBN: 978 1 4451 3021 7

Franklin Watts is a division of Hachette Children's Books, an Hachette UK company.
www.hachette.co.uk

Printed in China

Supplier 03, Date 0913, Print Run 2952
SL002125EN

Contents

What is War?

War is organized, armed conflict that takes place between nations, or between different people living within a nation. Countries waging war employ members of the military as combatants – soldiers, sailors or pilots, for example. Civil wars are fought between groups within the same state; these groups may be at war with one another for a range of reasons, but often because of their political, religious or ethnic differences. For thousands of years humans have both waged war and given lengthy consideration to the rights and wrongs – the ethics – of war.

The nature of war

Some wars are fought between two nations; for example, the Iran–Iraq War of 1980–8. But the nature of war means that it is prone to 'escalate', drawing in other countries. A network of alliances between countries meant that the two major wars of the 20th century, the First World War (1914–18) and the

An ongoing war

In 2001, as part of the 'war on terror', the United States (supported by British, Australian and Afghan troops) launched 'Operation Enduring Freedom' (OEF) in Afghanistan. One of the aims of this war was to destroy al-Qaeda, the terrorist organization held responsible for 9/11 (see page 7), which had its base in Afghanistan. OEF forces destroyed many of al-Qaeda's terrorist training camps and eventually (in 2011) tracked down and killed its leader, Osama bin Laden. Al-Qaeda, however, continues to operate. In 2012, US Defense Secretary Leon Panetta said that although he believed the 'war on terror' had significantly weakened al-Qaeda, the United States still had a '… responsibility to keep going after them [the terrorists] wherever they are.'

Second World War (1939–45), were waged between many different states. In the First World War, the Central Powers (Germany, Austria-Hungary, the Ottoman Empire and

Bulgaria) fought against the Allies (led by the Russian Empire, the British Empire, France and, from 1917, the United States). The Second World War was fought between the Allies (led by Britain, the Soviet Union and the United States) and the Axis Powers (led by Germany, Italy and Japan).

The 'war on terror'

In recent years, world events have made many people reconsider more traditional definitions of the word 'war'. On 11 September 2001, members of the Islamic extremist group al-Qaeda attacked major US institutions including the World Trade Center in New York City, and the Pentagon in Washington D.C., an event that has since become universally known by its date – 9/11. In response, US president George

W. Bush declared a 'war on terror' (see panel). By this he was implying a military campaign waged not against a specific nation or group, but against any extremist or terrorist organization that was considered a significant threat to US, and world, security.

Smoke billows from the twin towers of the World Trade Center in New York after the terrorist attack on the morning of 11 September, 2001. Both towers collapsed within two hours of being struck by the hijacked planes, with the loss of more than 2,000 lives.

The ethical arguments

When thinking about the ethics of war, the starting point for most people is that war is a bad thing because it involves deliberately killing or injuring people. War destroys lives and property, tears families apart and bankrupts national economies. It is dehumanizing and its effects can be felt long after the fighting has ceased. Nevertheless, nations praise their soldiers as heroes

The 1st Battalion of the Irish Guards march through Liverpool, UK, in 2008, on their return home from a tour of duty in Iraq. Members of the armed forces from nations such the United Kingdom and United States are involved in a wide variety of duties in countries across the world.

for their skill and bravery, and it does indeed take courage, loyalty and self-denial to be a member of the armed forces.

One way to reconcile the noble, self-sacrificing qualities of soldiering with the violent realities of war is to take the point of view that there are certain, well-defined circumstances in which war is morally acceptable. Some people, however, strongly believe that war is immoral and can never be justified – even in self-defence. Others insist that war is sometimes necessary and can be moral because the alternative – doing nothing while an evil tyrant invades other countries and commits mass murder, for example – is much worse.

Paper agreements

Ethical debates about war are an important part of the process of drawing up codes of war – rules that are agreed between countries (such as the Hague and Geneva conventions, see pages 24–5). Such debates also raise other questions: whether it is right to intervene in another country's affairs, for example; what the best practice might be for non-combatants such as journalists and photographers reporting on a war; or who has

Why do people go to war?

Three of the most common reasons for war are:

- **nationalism** – when people believe that their country is better than other countries (nationalism, religious belief and ethnic identity are sometimes linked)

- **militarism** – when governments aggressively build up military power in preparation for war

- **imperialism** – when one country forcibly takes control of another country (often for reasons of material gain – land, water, natural resources and so on)

responsibility for dealing with the aftermath of war.

Some people argue that whatever is agreed and signed on paper regarding moral conduct in war, skilled politicians can always manipulate the rules to fit their arguments. In other words, if a person or country is determined and has sufficient power to go to war, there is little that anyone can do to prevent it.

The history of war ethics

The moral questions surrounding war have been debated for thousands of years. The 'just war tradition', a theory that relies on a mutually agreed set of rules about war, is referred to in the Bible, in ancient Greek philosophy and in the ancient Indian epic tale,

Peaceful end?

'It is therefore with the desire for peace that wars are waged, even by those who take pleasure in exercising their warlike nature in command and battle. And hence it is obvious that peace is the end sought for by war.'

St Augustine of Hippo (354–430CE)

The *Mahabharata*. The ancient Roman statesman Cicero (106–43BCE) defined the conditions under which military force was justified, suggesting that it should be in proportion to the threat posed by the enemy. However, the practical and political issues that preoccupied ancient Greece and Rome tended to overwhelm any ethical concerns. In other words, wars were an extension of politics and were fought with great ruthlessness.

Christian views

The ideas of the early philosophers were developed by Christian thinkers. St Augustine said there were three just causes to go to war: self-defence; recapturing things taken; and punishing wrongdoers. St Thomas Aquinas (1225–74) discussed the kinds of activities that were permissible for a Christian in war. He wrote that war must only be fought for a good and just reason; should be declared by a properly instituted authority (such as the state); and that peace must be the central aim, even in the midst of violence. Later writers such as the

Spanish Renaissance philosopher Francisco de Vitoria (c.1486–1546) and the Dutch lawyer Hugo Grotius (1583–1645) built on these ideas.

A soldier's view

Carl von Clausewitz (1780–1831) was a professional soldier in the Prussian army and also a theorist – someone who was interested in examining and writing about all aspects of war. His book *On War* was published after his death and remains an important influence on military strategists to this day. He considered war to be an ever-changing and unstable combination of violent emotion, chance and rational calculation. In his writing he often presented both sides of a debate. For example his famous assertion that war is a 'continuation of policy by other means' was balanced by an earlier argument that 'war is nothing but a duel [a fight between two people] on a larger scale'.

(Opposite) Trajan's column (left) was completed in 113CE in Rome, to celebrate the victory of Emperor Trajan over the Dacian people in 106CE. The carvings on the column (right) show a wide range of military activities including marching, fighting battles and building forts.

11

Can War be Justified?

Is there such as thing as a 'just war'? If your country is invaded, or innocent civilians are targeted, do you have a moral duty to take up arms against the aggressor? Is it ever right to intervene in another country's affairs to prevent the spread of evil, or are good intentions an inadequate reason to wage war?

What is a just war?

Many people believe there are situations in which war is simply unavoidable. They say that in such cases war may be described as ethical, or 'just'. A war is only held to be just if the country or group wanting to use military force can prove there is a

A trigger for war

In 1941, an act of aggression without a formal declaration of war drew the United States into the Second World War. Tension between Japan and the United States had been building since the 1930s because of continued Japanese attacks on China. In 1941, Japan invaded Indochina (modern-day Cambodia, Laos and Vietnam). In response, the United States stopped oil exports to Japan. This forced the Japanese to act on plans to attack and take control of other oil-rich territories in southeast Asia – but first they needed to deal with the threat of the US naval fleet in the Pacific Ocean.

On 7 December 1941, Japanese fighter planes attacked the US Pacific Fleet at its naval base in Pearl Harbor, Hawaii. The attack was a terrible shock for the United States. The following day, US president Franklin D. Roosevelt asked Congress to declare war on Japan. Three days later, Japan's Axis allies (see page 7), Germany and Italy, declared war on the United States. Suddenly, the United States was at war, both in the Pacific and in Europe.

moral reason to do so and all forms of peaceful negotiation have failed.

The battleships USS *West Virginia* and USS *Tennessee* burn after the Japanese attack on Pearl Harbor, Hawaii. More than 2,000 US soldiers and sailors were killed in this surprise attack.

Acts of aggression

Probably the clearest example of a just cause for war is the defence of territory against invasion. Many people would argue that, in this circumstance, war is essential to avoid being dominated by a bullying nation which may then go on to invade other countries. Arguments for self-defence in other situations are less clear-cut. Some people say that attacking a nation's honour by, for example, assassinating (killing) its president or monarch or burning its flag is a just cause for war. Other people believe it is acceptable for a country to go to war if its religion is attacked, or if its economy is damaged by embargoes (bans) on trade. But many people say it is wrong to go to war for these reasons; they believe that such matters should be dealt with by peaceful and diplomatic means.

Lawful authority

A basic ethic of war is that any declaration of military action must be lawful. Today, many people consider the United Nations (UN) to be the only lawful authority for the declaration of war. The UN was established after the Second World War to maintain peace between nations and enforce international responsibilities. Its charter

Responsibilities

'The United Nations Security Council has not lived up to its responsibilities, so we will rise to ours.'

US President George W. Bush in a speech given on 17 March, 2003, the day before the invasion of Iraq

Negotiations at the United Nations Security Council in 1988 brought the war between Iran and Iraq to an end after nearly eight years of fighting.

allows the UN Security Council to 'determine the existence of any threat to the peace, breach of the peace, or act of aggression' and to take action to 'restore international peace and security'.

Disagreement over Korea

Despite UN involvement, there is often disagreement about whether wars have been lawfully declared. After the end of the Second World War, Korea was divided into two by the Allies (see page 7), with the communist Soviet Union in control of the northern half, and the United States in charge of the southern half. On 25 June 1950, North Korea, with the backing of the Soviet Union, invaded South Korea. The UN Security Council immediately condemned the invasion and two days later recommended that member states provide military assistance to South Korea.

The US president, Harry S. Truman, ordered air and sea forces to the region. But the Soviet Union argued that the US action was illegal because the Korean conflict was a civil war and beyond the scope of the UN Charter. The United States responded by saying that military action was essential to contain the spread of communism.

It was illegal

'I have indicated it [the invasion of Iraq] was not in conformity with [did not follow the rules of] the UN Charter. From our point of view, from the charter point of view, it was illegal.'

Kofi Annan,
Secretary-General
of the UN, 2004

UN resolutions

Since the 1990s, the UN has passed various resolutions to authorize the use of force, for example to expel Iraqi troops after the invasion of Kuwait (1990); and to allow the United States and UK to lead an invasion into Afghanistan to combat terrorism after 9/11 (see page 7). However, the invasion of Iraq in 2003 remains a controversial event. Some people believe that the United States and UK acted unethically in this case because they did not obtain a specific UN resolution before invading (see pages 26–7). Other people argue that there is no universal agreement as to how far the world's countries have given the UN their permission to authorize war. In practice, the power to declare war remains with individual states.

Humanitarian intervention

When is it right to intervene with military force in another country's affairs? Many people believe that such intervention is justified in cases of 'crimes against humanity'. These are crimes that violate people's most basic human rights – the right to life and liberty, the right not to be enslaved, the right not to be tortured. Crimes against humanity include atrocities and offences committed against civilian populations such as mass murder, or widespread persecution on political, racial or religious grounds.

Supporters of humanitarian intervention say that sometimes the use of force is the only way to prevent violence against innocent civilians, and to put right acts that 'shock the moral conscience of mankind' (an old legal expression). In these instances, they say, war is definitely the lesser of two evils. But some people say it is both immoral and illegal to respond to evil acts with deliberate violence. They argue that the idea of a just war deceives people into thinking that war is a 'good thing', and that this is never the case. They also fear that states

may claim humanitarian motives for intervention when in fact they have other, less praiseworthy incentives, for example, gaining access to natural resources such as oil.

Libya

In 2011, a NATO coalition (alliance of states) intervened in the civil war in Libya. The country was being torn apart by fighting between troops loyal to the government of Colonel Gaddafi, and rebels seeking to overthrow the government. Gaddafi had governed virtually unchallenged since seizing control of Libya by force in 1969. Over the years, the West had alternately done deals with Gaddafi and criticized him as a tyrant with links to terrorism. The NATO coalition justified its action by stating that the intervention was necessary to

Help and protection

'It's not a war – it's the only way to give our people the help and protection they need and have been asking for, to finish what they started.'

Jalal Shammam, spokesman for an anti-Gaddafi protest in London, 2011

protect civilians and to prevent a massacre (mass killing). Indeed, Gaddafi had warned that unless the rebels stopped their protests there would be 'rivers of blood'. But anti-war critics argued that the real motive for NATO action in Libya was greater power for the West in the region.

A poster in Tripoli, Libya, shows Colonel Muammar Gaddafi as heroic leader of his people. He was killed on 20 October 2011.

With good intention?

'War is the outcome, not mainly of evil intentions, but on the whole, of good intentions which miscarry or are frustrated. It is made, not usually by evil men knowing themselves to be wrong, but is the outcome of policies pursued by good men usually passionately convinced that they are right… ' (Norman Angell, winner of the Nobel Peace Prize, 1933). Most people would agree that 'evil intentions', such as seeking

A young Serb boy watches his house burn to the ground in Kosovo, in 1999. The bitter civil war in the region between ethnic Serbs and Albanians left many dead and thousands homeless.

power, or grabbing land or natural resources, cannot be used to justify war. Wars fought for bad motives usually lead to an unjust peace and further conflict. But what if the intentions of the aggressor are 'good' – if the aim of an attack is to restore or keep the peace, right a wrong or help the innocent?

Supporters say that good intentions may justify war as long as it is conducted in the right way; going to war may result in fewer casualties than simply sitting by and doing nothing. Opponents say unfortunately this is seldom the case and that 'good intentions which miscarry' can result in untold suffering.

The fog of war

Countries with good intentions may quickly find that these are abandoned in the 'fog of war'. War disrupts the normal rules of society; anger, fear and hatred make people regard the enemy as sub-human, morality becomes meaningless and terrible atrocities are committed. Furthermore, some countries may use good intentions as the reason for declaring war when really they disguise selfish motives. Some people have suggested that the 2003 war in Iraq

Kosovo

During the 1990s, there was civil war in the former Yugoslavia between the Serbian authorities and Albanians living in the province of Kosovo. The international community became increasingly concerned about the escalating conflict and its humanitarian consequences. In 1999, NATO launched a bombing campaign in an effort to stop the violence. Supporters argue that while this decisive action undoubtedly caused civilian deaths, it also averted more widespread bloodshed and brought the war to a swifter end. Opponents point out that it was not authorized by the UN Security Council, and argue that the bombing made both the violence and refugee situation worse.

was waged to further the economic interests of the United States in the Middle East rather than the stated aim of eliminating the threat posed by the Iraqi leader, Saddam Hussein, to his own people and to the world at large (see page 26–7).

A last resort?

Should war always be the last resort, after every other alternative has been tried? Some people argue that, although war is the least preferred course of action, it should not necessarily be avoided until every other alternative has failed. They say that, in some circumstances, not declaring war early on only allows an enemy to build up resources. This means that a war may ultimately be more destructive.

Diplomacy and sanctions

A wide range of strategies is used by nations to try to solve international issues without resorting to war. Diplomacy – negotiations carried out between countries by their representatives – is going on all the time, but can be particularly important at times of international tension. If the government of a particular country is acting in a way that causes international concern, other nations can put pressure on that country through economic sanctions – restrictions on trade and finance. These can include banning or taxing trade in particular products, or the withdrawal of financial aid. The UN Security Council also has the power to impose sanctions. However, some people argue that sanctions can be

Talk not war

'To jaw-jaw [talk] is always better than to war-war.'

Remark made by Sir Winston Churchill, British prime minister during the Second World War, at a lunch in the White House, Washington D.C. in 1954

as damaging to a country as warfare. They point out that it is usually the civilian population that suffers when sanctions lead to shortages of vital supplies. Worse, they say that it is the poor, sick, young and elderly who are mostly affected.

The rule of double effect

What if an action taken in war to hasten a particular 'good' outcome also results, to a far lesser extent, in the opposite outcome? When this occurs, it is known as the rule of double effect. For example, some people believe it would be acceptable to bomb an enemy's headquarters, even though civilians in the surrounding area might also be killed. They hold this view because they consider the good effect of destroying the headquarters and probably bringing a swifter end to the war (with fewer

Sooner than later

'If you want to avoid a very big and very bad war later, be prepared to fight a small and principled war now…'

Christopher Hitchens, British–American author and journalist, 'Just Give Peace a Chance?', 2011

casualties) outweighs the bad effect of possible civilian deaths from the bombing (so-called 'collateral damage'). However, many people argue that it is never acceptable to cause harm – intentionally or otherwise.

Fresh produce on sale in a market in Baghdad, Iraq, in 1999. International sanctions on Iraq after its invasion of Kuwait in 1990 led to shortages of some food, medicines and other supplies.

A good chance of success

According to another 'just war' principle, a state should go to war only if it has a good chance of winning. If there is little chance of a good outcome then it is unethical to wage war because it will bring immeasurable suffering to innocent civilians. But the logical extension of this argument implies that poorer or smaller states should never go to war because they are unlikely to achieve victory.

Against alliances

'I know that military alliances and armament have been the reliance for peace for centuries, but they do not produce peace; and when war comes, as it inevitably does under such conditions, these armaments and alliances but intensify and broaden the conflict.'

From a speech given by US politician Frank B. Kellogg, who was awarded the Nobel Peace Prize in 1929

One way in which less powerful states can improve their chances of success is to work together to defeat a common enemy. In 1939, at the beginning of the Second World War, Great Britain was faced with the proposition of taking on the much larger and better-prepared forces of Nazi Germany. With apparently little chance of success, it could be argued that to go to war in this case was unethical. But Britain did eventually triumph, mainly because other countries with greater wealth at their disposal, such as the United States, joined the conflict on its side.

International loyalties

Although alliances between countries help small and weak states to stand up to large ones, such alliances can also draw countries into war. Again, the events of 1939 provide a useful example. Faced with increasing aggression from Nazi Germany, both Britain and France promised to come to Poland's aid if Germany invaded. In fact, when Germany

Welcome ally

'No American will think it wrong of me if I proclaim that to have the United States at our side was to me the greatest joy. I could not foretell the course of events… but now at this very moment I knew the United States was in the war, up to the neck and in to the death. So we had won after all!'

Winston Churchill, in 1950, describing his reaction after the Pearl Harbor attack brought the United States into the Second World War

did attack Poland on 1 September there was little Britain or France could do on the ground, but two days later both countries declared war on Germany. Germany's aggression, followed by the response of Britain and France, plunged Europe into the Second World War. Many people would say that if countries make agreements then it is a matter of honour to stick to them. Others argue that such alliances are inherently dangerous because they can trigger 'chain reactions'.

Allies in wartime: a poster from the Second World War shows US president Franklin D. Roosevelt (left) and the British prime minister Winston Churchill. Also illustrated are the flags of the Allies (see page 7), and the sinking of the Japanese battleship *Haruna*.

Waging War

Throughout history, rules about the conduct of war have been written down by monarchs, politicians and military strategists. These rules are intended to govern behaviour and breaking them is seen as a crime. But many people say that written rules have only limited influence and tend to be abandoned on the battlefield.

The conduct of war is about *how* rather than *why* a war should be fought. It covers issues such as who it is ethical to fight, how much force should be used, whether certain weapons should be used, and the role of international conventions on war.

Military conduct

For hundreds of years, military behaviour in wartime was based on unwritten understandings between opponents. From the 19th century onwards, the international community has made efforts to introduce legal limits on the conduct of war by drawing up treaties (agreements) between various countries. In 1864, 12 governments signed the first Geneva Convention, agreeing to give protection to hospitals and their staff, as well as to civilians helping the wounded.

Conventions

1864 the first Geneva Convention is signed in Switzerland

1899 the first Hague Convention focuses on disarmament efforts

1906 the second Geneva Convention gives protection to wounded combatants at sea

1907 the second Hague Convention states that war should not commence without previous warning by a government with the authority to declare war

1929 the third Geneva Convention lays down rules to protect prisoners of war

1949 the fourth Geneva Convention adds rules to protect civilians during war

Soldiers taking part in a military training exercise learn how to operate in an urban area.

In 1899 and 1907, two international treaties were negotiated at peace conferences at The Hague in the Netherlands. The Hague Conventions focused on the laws of war and war crimes, and aimed to create an international court where disputes between countries could be resolved. However, many of the rules laid down at the Hague Conventions were soon violated in the First World War.

Central principles

Today international law binds countries together in an attempt to regulate and limit the methods of warfare. It aims to strike a balance between military action and the reduction of human suffering, particularly among civilians. There are several main principles underlying the laws of war. First, war should be limited to achieving the political goals that started the war and should not include unnecessary destruction. Secondly, wars should be brought to an end as quickly as possible. Thirdly, people and property that do not contribute to the war effort should be protected against unnecessary destruction and hardship.

Pre-emptive strikes

A pre-emptive strike is military action taken by a country in response to a threat from another country without a formal declaration of war. But is it ethical to go to war because of the strong likelihood or threat of an attack? Pre-emptive strikes raise many other ethical questions, too. A just war should be a last resort (see page 20–1) – but a pre-emptive strike does not usually allow for attempts at diplomacy or other peaceful alternatives. And if one nation launches a pre-emptive strike without the formalities of declaring war, does that open the door to other nations doing exactly the same?

The Six-Day War

One of the most famous pre-emptive strikes in history was in June 1967, when Israel launched a surprise attack against Egypt, Syria and Jordan. In the months leading up to this attack, Egypt in particular had taken many actions that appeared to threaten Israel, including moving thousands of troops into Sinai, the border area between Israel and Egypt. Despite diplomatic efforts to calm the growing crisis, the Israeli government decided that military

Justification

'…[Saddam Hussein's] weapons of mass destruction programme is active, detailed and growing… it is up and running now.'

Tony Blair, British prime minister, speaking in support of the invasion of Iraq in 2003

action was necessary. In military terms, the brief (six-day) war that followed was a success for Israel, because the Israelis captured areas of great strategic importance. However, the bitterness of defeat felt by the Arab states sowed the seeds for the territorial, religious and ethnic struggles that continue in the region to this day.

War in Iraq

Another problem with a pre-emptive strike is that it turns the side carrying out the strike into the aggressor. In 2003, the United States and its allies took pre-emptive action against the government of Saddam Hussein in Iraq. The main justification given for this strike was the presence of weapons of mass destruction (WMD, see page

30) in Iraq which, it was claimed, posed a threat to world peace. Although the war toppled Saddam Hussein's regime, it cost thousands of civilian lives and in the end no WMD were ever found. Critics of the war argued that such a policy of 'strike first, ask questions later' was extremely dangerous because it might encourage other countries to ignore internationally agreed rules, resulting in a more unstable and violent world.

Demonstrators outside the United States Capitol building in Washington D.C. in 2007 protest at the ongoing conflict in Iraq.

Perils of pre-emption

'A global strategy based on the new Bush doctrine [policy] of pre-emption means the end of the system of international institutions, laws and norms [rules] that we have worked to build for more than half a century.'

William Galston,
'Perils of Preemptive War', 2002

Proportionality

As a general rule, the methods and means used in military action must be in proportion to the military objective. The force used should be sufficient to win, but should not be excessive. A battle must end before it becomes a massacre; and it is unethical to kill the soldiers of an army that has surrendered. All sound principles, of course, but difficult to enforce in the heat of war. Some people say that the decision to wage war is governed by realism and relative strength, not ethics. They argue that ideas of moral behaviour are very low on the agenda and trying to enforce them is pointless and unrealistic; in a conflict, the saying goes, 'the strong do what they will and the weak do what they must'.

The Geneva Convention forbids attacks on civilians, including the bombing of areas in which civilians may be present. During the 20th century, however, new methods of waging war resulted in increasingly higher proportions of civilian deaths. In the Second World War, for example, large numbers of civilian casualties resulted from bombing carried out by both British and German airforces. Overall, in the Second World War, more than half of all casualties were civilians. More recently, highly sophisticated technology has allowed military forces to launch so-called 'surgical strikes'. These are attacks that are intended to damage or destroy a military target, with little or no destruction beyond the target. Many people doubt that these strikes are as 'clean' as they are

Combatants and non-combatants

Who is it ethical to fight in a war? Combatants, members of the armed forces who play a direct part in hostilities, are thought to be legitimate targets. Non-combatants – for example, medical staff and military chaplains who do not take a direct part in the fighting – are not thought to be legitimate targets.

Humane and effective

'Our air strikes were the most effective, yet humane, in the history of warfare.'

President George H.W. Bush, discussing the Gulf War (following the Iraqi invasion of Kuwait) in May 1991

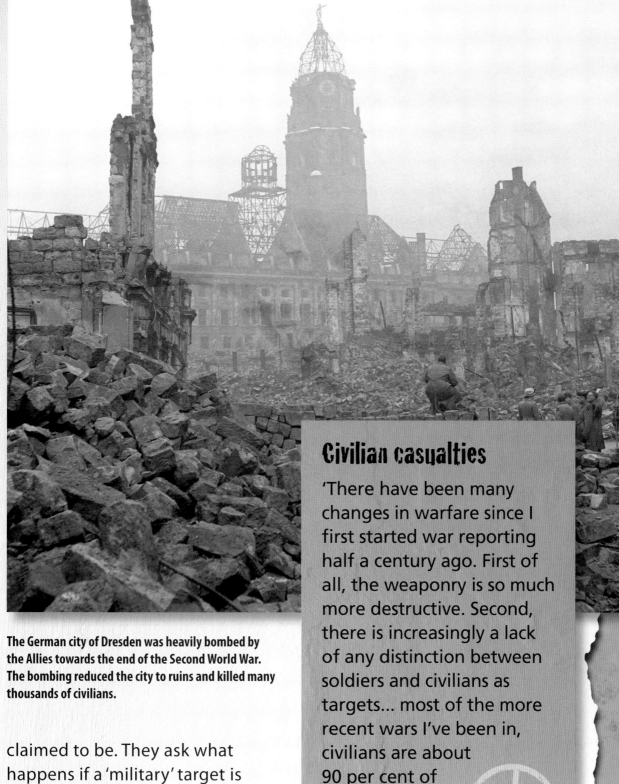

The German city of Dresden was heavily bombed by the Allies towards the end of the Second World War. The bombing reduced the city to ruins and killed many thousands of civilians.

Civilian casualties

'There have been many changes in warfare since I first started war reporting half a century ago. First of all, the weaponry is so much more destructive. Second, there is increasingly a lack of any distinction between soldiers and civilians as targets... most of the more recent wars I've been in, civilians are about 90 per cent of the casualties.'

Martin Bell, BBC war correspondent, 2009

claimed to be. They ask what happens if a 'military' target is wrongly identified? And what happens if the military target just happens to be situated in the middle of a civilian area?

Weapons

Rules about the choice of weapons in war are a major part of the law on the conduct of hostilities. Certain types of weapons have been outlawed through a series of international treaties. They include so-called 'weapons of mass destruction' (WMD) – nuclear, chemical and biological weapons – which have the capacity to harm large numbers of people. Other weapons covered by these treaties include lasers that are designed to cause permanent blindness, and anti-personnel landmines, small devices buried just beneath the surface of the ground that explode when someone steps on them. The issue of landmines is particularly controversial because they remain in place after a war has ended. As a result they continue to kill and maim civilians, and put large areas of valuable land out of use, often for many decades after the end of hostilities.

Atom bombs

How do WMD fit into the theory of a just war? If a whole nation is 'at war' is it ethical to use mass bombing or nuclear attack to instill terror, and possibly bring

Risking lives

'According to the just war principles, it is better to risk the lives of one's own combatants than the lives of enemy non-combatants.'

The Christian Century, *pointing out one of the ethical problems raised by the use of drones, 2010*

the war to a quicker end? On 6 and 9 August 1945, the United States dropped two atom bombs on the Japanese cities of Hiroshima and Nagasaki. The terrible destruction and loss of life resulted in Japan's rapid surrender and an end to the Second World War in the Pacific (the war in Europe ended in May 1945). The role of the bombings and their ethical justification are debated to this day.

Unmanned weapons

A more recent development is the use of unmanned weapons (drones). These include aircraft that can be used to spy on enemy territory, watch and identify enemy movements and bases, and ultimately attack enemies on the ground without risking any lives on the attacking side. Some people argue that drones result in greater precision and less 'collateral damage'. Others say that they make it far too easy for an aggressor to wage war from a vast, and safe, distance.

An unmanned aerial vehicle (UAV), more commonly known as a drone. UAVs can be controlled from many thousands of miles away, far from enemy territory.

Accountable

'I am ultimately accountable… for somebody who is not on the battlefield who got killed… and so we do not take that lightly… we have an interest in reducing civilian casualties because I don't want civilians killed.'

US President Barack Obama, speaking at a news conference in 2010

War and Religion

The world's main religions all preach compassion and justice, but they have also been at the heart of many wars in history. In the last century, politics and foreign policy took centre stage in the two world wars and it seemed as though wars of religion had become a thing of the past. However, since then, religion has once more played a central role. Why is this, and is it ever ethical to go to war under the banner of faith?

A cause worth fighting for?

In the last 40 years, religious differences have been the reason for conflict in parts of the world including Lebanon, Northern Ireland, Sri Lanka, the former Yugoslavia and Nigeria. However, economic or political issues (for example, tribal disputes over territory) are often at the heart of many so-called religious wars.

Does religious conviction justify warlike behaviour? For many people, the idea of killing and injuring people in war has no place in any religious faith. Some people believe that when wars develop a religious perspective (for example, if people insist that God says they have a right to a certain piece of land) they are more difficult to resolve.

Religious rules

The moral rules laid down by religion can seem contradictory when it comes to war. Modern Christians believe that war is rarely acceptable though it may be necessary (in the form of a 'just war') as a tool to promote peace and justice. Judaism accepts that certain kinds of war are ethically justified and that it is sometimes morally acceptable to kill people.

Hinduism's doctrine of *ahimsa* condemns violence and war, but its warrior class (*Kshatriya*) permits war; Hindus believe it is right to use force in self-defence. Like Christians, many Sikhs believe in the concept of 'just war' (*Dharam Yudh*), but they also think that, if a war is just, it should be undertaken even if it cannot be won. Islam regards war as a last resort. Buddhists oppose war and believe that violence is never a way to end conflict – although the mostly Buddhist Sinhalese population was involved in the civil war in Sri Lanka.

Flash of steel

'When all efforts to restore peace prove useless and no words avail,
Lawful is the flash of steel,
It is right to draw
the sword.'

Words of Guru Gobind Singh, the tenth Sikh guru

Two young Tamil Tiger fighters in Sri Lanka, in 1991. The Tamil Tigers were formed in 1976 to fight for an independent homeland in the north of the island. The war also had a religious context – the Tamil minority in Sri Lanka are mostly Hindu, while the Sinhalese majority are largely Buddhist.

Holy wars

Holy wars usually have three elements: a religious goal; authorization by a religious leader; and the promise of a spiritual reward for the participants. For a war to be a holy war, religion has to be the driving force.

Jihad

The word *jihad* means 'struggle'. Muslims use it to describe three things: a believer's internal struggle to live as devoutly as possible according to Islam; the external struggle to

The siege of Jerusalem during the First Crusade (1096-9). The Crusaders made siege weapons, shown here, to attack the impressive walls of the city.

The Crusades

The Crusades were a series of Christian holy wars waged between 1095 and 1291. The battleground was the Holy Land – the region around Jerusalem which was an important place of worship for Muslims, Christians and Jews. From the 7th century, this region had been under the control of Muslim rulers who allowed both Christians and Jews access to their holy sites. But in the 1070s the routes used by Christian pilgrims to the Holy Land were disrupted. In 1095, the leader of the Roman Catholic Church, Pope Urban II, called for a holy war to recapture Jerusalem. He described all those who fought as 'soldiers of God'. But when the Christian invaders finally captured Jerusalem in 1099, they slaughtered hundreds of Muslim and Jewish residents in the city.

build a good Muslim society; and the struggle to defend Islam with force, if necessary. When Muslims or their faith or territory are attacked, Islam permits them to wage war in self-defence. In recent years, however, some Islamist extremists have used *jihad* to describe a 'holy war' involving attacks on Western targets (such as 9/11).

Islam emphasizes that war should be avoided and only fought for noble motives. It states that *jihad* should not involve the conversion of people to Islam, nor should it be used to conquer and colonize other nations. However, some Muslim thinkers interpret the teachings of the Qur'an, Islam's holy book, differently. They say it contains 'sword verses' which justify war against unbelievers as a tool to spread Islam. An even more extreme interpretation says that non-Muslims are 'enemies of God' against whom it is legitimate to use violence.

Inter-faith dialogue

Most people believe that warlike developments in religious thinking should be challenged. They say that dialogue should exist between faiths to try to reach better understanding and to increase acceptance of others. In 2007, 138 Muslim scholars and clerics joined together to declare the common ground between Christianity and Islam. Does dialogue make a difference or not? Some people believe that this is the best strategy for defence against war; others say that inter-faith dialogue has always existed – but so has war.

Pacifism

For some people, war is never justified. Absolute pacifists believe it is wrong to take part in war, even in self-defence. But how does this argument work on a political level if a country finds itself under attack?

Different types of pacifism

Absolute pacifists believe war is wasteful and that nothing can justify killing a person deliberately. They think violence always produces worse results than non-violence. They may even argue that violence should not be used to rescue an innocent person who is being attacked and could be killed. This is a very difficult moral position to hold.

Pacifists generally reject the idea that there is any such thing as a 'just war'. But conditional pacifists accept that sometimes war is preferable to the alternative. Other types of pacifist may only oppose wars involving weapons of mass destruction, pointing out that from a logical point of view such conflicts are likely to end in total destruction and are therefore unwinnable. Many pacifists actively promote peaceful ways of settling conflict.

There is an element of pacifism in many religious teachings – Buddhism and Jainism both strongly promote pacifist beliefs. While Christianity generally supports the just war theory, there are groups within the Christian faith, such as Quakers, who are active pacifists.

Self-defence

'The first thing which was striking is this, that the same causes and reasons for the war were heard everywhere. Each warring nation solemnly assured you it is fighting under the impulse of self-defense.'

Jane Addams, US social reformer and pacifist, speaking against the United States' entry into the First World War, 1915

Pacifists in wartime

In wartime, pacifists may refuse to fight. Instead they may choose to carry out tasks that contribute to the national good, for example working as cooks, on farms, or as ambulance

Peace protesters in Washington D.C. march to the Pentagon in 2009 as part of an anti-war demonstration.

drivers or medical workers. During the First World War, some pacifists in the UK refused to play any part in the conflict and were imprisoned for their beliefs.

Opponents of pacifism say that while it may appease an individual's conscience to believe in peace at any price, pacifism cannot be used at a national level. They argue that it would be irresponsible and immoral for a government to refuse to defend its citizens in the face of an aggressor.

An advantage to others

'There is no avoiding war; it can only be postponed to the advantage of others.'

Niccolò Machiavelli, political scientist and writer (1469–1527)

Non-violence

Modern ideas about non-violence have their roots in the actions taken by the Indian leader, Mohandas Gandhi, who led the movement against British rule in his country in the first half of the 20th century. Gandhi's doctrine of non-violence was based on his interpretation

This stamp, printed in India, commemorates the centenary of the birth of Mohandas Gandhi in 1869. Gandhi's use of non-violent protest inspired similar movements all over the world.

Undermining the opponent

'Non-violent action provides a way of acting effectively in a conflict without the use of physical violence... While non-violent forms of struggle do not kill, injure, or destroy, they undermine an opponent's social, economic, political, and military power by withholding and withdrawing the pillars of support required by an adversary [enemy] to maintain its position and to achieve its goals.'

From the website of the Albert Einstein Institution

of the Hindu principle of *ahimsa* (see page 33). This covered three main beliefs: first, that people find it difficult to kill or harm others, especially if they have a personal connection with them. Secondly, people are less likely to kill or harm others if they are watched by someone who challenges their behaviour. Thirdly, leaders who want to wage war rely on the support and effort of others to carry out their orders. While pacifism rejects the use of violence but does not necessarily promote change, non-violent action is usually linked with the intention of bringing about social or political change.

A violent solution?

'Violence is like money: it can't make you happy, save your soul, make you a better person – but it certainly can solve things. When the winners exterminate [kill] the losers, historical conflicts are permanently solved.'

D. A. Clarke, US feminist and writer, 1991

In practice

Non-violence includes acts of protest and civil disobedience, such as peaceful protests, pickets (demonstrations near targeted events), and vigils (peaceful gatherings to mark a specific event). The aim is often to raise public awareness of an issue and to try to convert opponents – to win hearts and minds. Non-violent action organizations work to reverse the 'desensitizing' effects of military training – to encourage soldiers to feel compassion for others and think for themselves. They arrange support for people or communities who might be targeted in war. They also encourage dialogue between conflicting groups.

Impractical?

Some people argue that the concept of non-violence is both idealistic and impractical. They say it is all very well to preach non-violence, but people who practise violence use it for a reason – because it is effective. They argue that as the powerful use violence to hold on to their power, the only way to counter it is also to use violence, even if this is only one of a range of different tactics.

Aftermath

Be prepared

'To be prepared for war is one of the most effective means of preserving peace.'

George Washington (1732–99), first president of the United States

War ends when one side has been defeated and the other is victorious, or both sides agree to a ceasefire. But who is responsible for dealing with the aftermath of war? What are the ethical questions to be considered when drawing up peace settlements? And how should war crimes be prosecuted?

Time and again throughout history a victorious nation has exploited its defeated opponent by taking territory, property and natural resources, or by imposing new political or religious frameworks. However, 'just war' theory supports the idea that moral principles should be observed following the end of war, not only for reasons of justice but also to avoid the anger and unrest that may result from harsh measures. As an example, many people consider the agreement that was drawn up after the First World War (the Treaty of Versailles, 1919) to have excessively punished the defeated Germany. They say that this unjust peace, and the resentment it caused, contributed to the eventual outbreak of the Second World War.

Justice after war

For those who believe in just war theory there are various issues to be taken into account after the end of a conflict. An aggressor should not be allowed to hold on to unjust gains, for example captured territory. There must be security for the 'victim' against any future attack. Civilians in the aggressor country should not be punished (unless they have committed human rights violations).

Some people argue that, in recent years, developments in military technology have allowed powerful countries such as the United States to win wars relatively easily – for example the toppling of Saddam Hussein's government in Iraq (see pages 26-7). These critics point out, however, that less consideration is given to 'winning the peace' in the aftermath of these wars. Military forces often remain in a defeated country to oversee the transition to peace. Their job is to help re-establish order and to rebuild the country. In the case of civil war, they may often have to negotiate between people who were recently fighting each other. Some people argue that such peace-keeping operations are essential; others say they are an unnecessary drain on the resources of the international community.

War is terrorism

'We need to decide that we will not go to war, whatever reason is conjured up by the politicians or the media, because war in our time is always indiscriminate, a war against innocents, a war against children. War is terrorism, magnified a hundred times.'

Howard Zinn, US historian and activist, 2001

A soldier with the United Nations Protection Force (UNPROFOR) in Bosnia carries an injured woman to a medical centre in 1994. UNPROFOR peace-keeping troops were in operation in Croatia and Bosnia-Herzegovina from 1992 until 1995.

War crimes

The concept of war crimes – the idea that individuals can be held responsible for the actions of a country or its military forces – is a relatively recent one. Until the Second World War, it was generally accepted that atrocities were part of the nature of war. But the systematic murder of several million people, mainly Jews, by Nazi Germany, and the mistreatment of civilians and prisoners of war by the Japanese during the Second World War, led to a drive to prosecute war criminals under international law. In 1945 and 1946, war crimes trials in Nuremberg, Germany, resulted in the executions of 12 Nazi leaders. A similar process began in Japan in 1948.

Who goes on trial?

Those on trial include leaders who have taken part in any of the specific crimes listed under international law (see panel). The people who are tried for war crimes are usually from the losing side. A victorious nation seldom tries its own people for war crimes. Some people argue that the trials can look like revenge trials and be seen as acts of injustice.

Defendants often say that they were obeying orders given by a superior, so were not responsible for the crimes. This argument may be taken into consideration and can result in a less harsh sentence, but it does not mean the defendants will avoid

War crimes

Under the terms of the Rome Statute (1998) the International Criminal Court can prosecute the following crimes:

- *genocide* acts committed with intent to destroy, in whole or in part, a national, ethnic, racial or religious group

- *crimes against humanity* atrocities against the civilian population, including murder, enslavement, deportation, torture, rape or persecution on political, racial or religious grounds

- *war crimes* atrocities or offences against people or property which violate the laws or customs of war

- *crimes of aggression* the use of armed force by a state against the sovereignty, territory or political independence of another state

International flags near the Yugoslavia Tribunal building in The Hague, the Netherlands. This tribunal is prosecuting war crimes committed in the former Yugoslavia.

punishment. The same argument applies for those pleading old age or ill-health. Some people say that compassion should be shown in these instances; others insist that the nature of these crimes is so serious that it does not make any difference how old or ill the defendant is.

International court

For many years, members of international human rights groups called for a global legal system to deal with war crimes. In 2002, a permanent International Criminal Court was set up at The Hague in the Netherlands. Opponents of the idea say the court could be used to pursue politically motivated prosecutions. But supporters say it is a significant development in the right direction.

Glossary

aggressor the person or group doing the attacking; the attacker

alliance a close association of nations or other groups

civil war a war fought between rival groups within the same state

civilians people who are not active members of the military

coalition a union of countries that stand together, for example, to fight a war

collateral coinciding or accompanying

combatant someone who takes a direct part in armed conflict, for example, a member of the armed forces of a country

communism a system of government in which the state controls the economy and private ownership is abolished

democracy a system of government in which the people elect politicians to represent them

doctrine a system of beliefs

embargo a government ban on trade with a foreign nation

escalate to increase in an uncontrolled manner

ethics the rights and wrongs of a subject

ethnic describes a group of people who share the same racial, national, religious, or cultural origin

extremist describes groups or ideas that are far outside ('extreme') what is considered normal and acceptable by the majority of people

genocide the deliberate attempt to murder everyone from a particular ethnic group

humanitarian describes action that is designed to save lives, help suffering and maintain human dignity

Nazi a supporter of the far-right beliefs of the political party that gained control of Germany in the 1930s under the leadership of Adolf Hitler

non-combatant someone not directly involved in military conflict; a civilian

North Atlantic Treaty Organization (NATO) an international organization established in 1949, made up of states which agree to defend one another in the event of military attack

Ottoman Empire a Turkish empire that lasted from 1299 until 1923

persecution severe mistreatment of an individual or group, often because of different political or religious beliefs

philosopher someone who studies or writes about the meaning of life

pre-emptive describes an action taken as a measure against something possible, anticipated, or feared

rape any act of sex that is forced upon a person without their consent

resolution in the United Nations, a formal statement of a decision

sanctions restrictions on trade and finance imposed by one country, or group of countries, on another

sovereignty royal rank, power or authority

Soviet Union (USSR) a huge communist state that existed between 1922 and 1990 – now the Russian Federation

strategist someone experienced in military planning

surgical strike a precise military attack on a specific target

United Nations an international organization founded in 1945 to maintain peace and security around the world and to promote human rights

violate to assault or harm

Further information

Books

Ethical Debates: Military Intervention Kaye Stearman, Wayland, 2012

Living Through: The Gulf Wars With Iraq Jane Bingham, Heinemann Library, 2012

Opposing Viewpoints: War Crimes Margaret Haerens, Greenhaven Press, 2010

Our World Divided: Afghanistan From War to Peace Philip Steele, Wayland, 2011

Voices Against War: A Century of Protest Lyn Smith, Mainstream Publishing Company, 2009

Websites

http://www.aeinstein.org
The Albert Einstein Institution website lists 198 methods of non-violent action, together with case studies

http://www.bbc.co.uk/ethics/war
The BBC's ethics site offers clear and concise information about aspects of war, just war theory, religious attitudes and pacifism

http://www.carnegiecouncil.org
An educational institution, the Carnegie Council offers resources on ethics in war and peace

http://www.icc-cpi.int/Menus/ICC/Home
Website of the International Criminal Court in The Hague, the Netherlands

http://www.iep.utm.edu/war/
The Internet Encyclopedia of Philosophy has sections on war and just war theory

http://www.ifrc.org/
The International Federation of Red Cross and Red Crescent Societies is the world's largest humanitarian and development network. It works to address the various forms of violence that deny individuals' rights to safety, health and human dignity. The site offers examples of non-violent intervention in war-torn communities.

Index

Bold entries indicate pictures

Both Sides of the Story
SERIES CONTENTS

Animal Rights Different from us? • Without feeling? • Do they have rules? • A background to animal rights • Practising what you preach? • Meat, milk and mass-production • Factory farming • Good farming? • Animal products • Animals and science • Genetic engineering • Wild animals • Culling • The pleasure principle • Four-legged friends • Animals in entertainment • Hunting • Rights and wrongs • The way forward

The Arab-Israeli Conflict What are the historical claims? • Zionism and Arab nationalism • Seeds of dissent • The Jewish state • Victory or catastrophe? • At war • The aftermath • The October War • The Palestine Liberation Organization • Freedom fighters or terrorists? • The 'occupied territories' • First Intifada • Talking peace? • Oslo Accords and after • The Second Intifada • The security fence • Core issues • The refugee question • Two-state solution?

Cloning and Genetic Engineering What is genetic engineering? • History of genetic engineering • Human Genome Project • Transgenics • Cloning • Animal and human cloning • Research cloning • Genetic engineering in medicine • Genetic testing • Gene therapy • Embryo testing • Saviour siblings • Pharming • The future of medical treatment? • Food and farming • GM animals and crops • GM in our food • Wider uses of genetic engineering • Sport

The Death Penalty A suitable punishment? • The view worldwide • How is it enforced? • The death penalty in history • The movement for abolition • Some religious views • 'Thou shalt not kill'? • Retribution or vengeance? • Justice for the victim? • Life in prison • Does it stop crime? • Is it cost-effective? • Who is executed? • A poor person's punishment? • Race and the death penalty • Who should not be executed? • Case studies • Competency • Abolition or not?

The Ethics of War What is war? • The ethical arguments • The history of war ethics • Can war be justified? • Lawful authority • Humanitarian intervention • With good intention? • A last resort? • A good chance of success • Waging war • Pre-emptive strikes • Proportionality • Weapons • War and religion • Holy wars • Pacifism • Non-violence • Aftermath • War crimes

Euthanasia A matter of life and death • Different types of euthanasia • A noble end? • An end to suffering? • The practice of medicine • Life support • Mental anguish • Euthanasia and old age • The role of relatives • Safeguards and living wills • The role of religion • Do not kill? • Euthanasia and the law • 'Suicide tourism' • The 'slippery slope' • Palliative care • The uncertainty principle • A time to die? • *On Death and Dying*